WALKING
*H*OME

WALKING HOME

Returning to the Pembrokeshire Coast

GWYNE HOWELL JAMES

To order additional copies of this book, contact:
Xlibris
800-056-3182
www.Xlibrispublishing.co.uk
Orders@Xlibrispublishing.co.uk
762752

Contents

1. Great Beginnings Amroth—Tenby 1

2. Whiteout Tenby—Freshwater East 7

3. Bionomic Thrum Freshwater East—Freshwater West 11

4. Walking Home Freshwater West—Kilpaison Bay 15

5. Genuflect Skeletons Kilpaison Bay—Pembroke Dock 19

6. Towns and Industry Pembroke Dock—Sandy Haven 23

7. Transformative Vortex Sandy Haven—St Anne's Head 27

8. Homo Sapien Accommodation
   St Anne's Head-Martin's Haven 31

9. Modest Acumen Martin's Haven—Broad Haven 35

10. A History Lesson Broad Haven—Newgale 39

11. Residuum Chattel Newgale—St David's 43

12. Counting the Stars St David's—White Sands Bay 47

13. Some Profanities White Sands Bay—Porthgain 51

14. Afflatus to Write Porthgain—Carn Ogof 55

15. Rock Cycles Carn Ogof—Goodwick 59

16. Specular Reflection Goodwick—Cwm yr Eglwys 63

17. Fifty Shades Cwm-yr-Eglwys—Ceibwr Bay 67

18. Embracing the End Ceibwr Bay—St Dogmaels 73

1. Great Beginnings Amroth—Tenby

the early flooding trickling bubbling sea gently ribbing the flat sands, the phon of ravenous squawking seagulls over me struggling to don my bland walking garb in a cheerless October morning drizzle, senses awakening prickling, troubling me, I moan and grizzle yet I planned this feat of certitude for the seasonal solitude, trying to balance amid the dawning against the car boot on gravel and stone in stocking'd feet still yawning chilly, damp and soggy, frail and timorous ahead lays hilly ramp and boggy dale the continuous drone of oceanic soundings to my left,

the moment of truth the here and now upon us, deftly I conquer the first step on a momentous journey planned in my youth forty odd years prior, it's to be my EFT, I turn and take a moment to suss my surroundings, the shore at Amroth great beginnings dramatic, portentous, I light my friendly old briar pipe, with my Rush 25 bag on the backpack type passing the local over bladderwrack, spall and stone where last summer I drank all of a flagon, with Paula and Mairwen, of 'double dragon',

the damp flag, *Baner Cymru* pummelling in a glum sideswipe squall of high wind, up the slope here is a stumm medieval castle come mansion whose halls served as an asylum during the empires bedlam hype, I fished for tope all along this flipe anticline faulted ridge towards the wall at Wiseman's Bridge in the fall of the hopeful late sixties with Eric, lately he's *not* well or is that polemics altogether he's definitely under the weather,

In the mid nineteen thirties Sir Cedric Morris made his start to ply his art from this Inn on pony *and* cart along this coastal park, here then lays my quest or question, I reach the cover of the rising past the car park where, still surprising, jeep and wagons with adventurers inside them yoke canoe and surfboard awaiting the tide and foaming wash of beach breakers

behind the council WCs a ruddy, muddy staircase span aspiring to
Tinkers Hill I climb the crest that saps my legs and my breath I take a
rest acquiring Rodin's 'thinker' vigil, looking back over the bay's
coastally sleepy, pleasing vision, on low tide the ghostly, creepy
teasing scission of a forest petrified long ago can be seen yet
relatively not so long ago the set would have been a bustling sight at
its height a hive of activity steam clouds of engines as grey crowds of
dysphoric grey skinned miners with reluctant, gainful objectivity
traverse to a seam of superior, blessed anthracite godsend and curse,
preferred by Queen Victoria no less.

I turn and take the hill with stretched legs and second breath
through the field past the caravan park and at length to Wiseman's
Bridge, I bustle down along the macule shore more cobbles, shingle
and scree, reflective in the myriad mussel bound rock pools I glimpse
a scene from forty three, Monty and Winston overseeing operation
Jantzen preparations for the beginning of the end landings on gold I
climb back to the path upon the wall passed the old mine-working
'caban' or den by way of the tunnels to Coppet Hall along what was
back then the rail track carrying miners and coal,

just up the road near Stepaside through Pleasant Valley remnants lurk
of Kilgetty iron works, I walked that path into the coppice earlier
last year to escape the office and gape the ambience of deep wood
calm with its singular Grace-ful penillion, after the second tunnel the
world enlarges on the 'Coast's' most largess parking lot where I take
a minute looking back from whither I set out, on the sea a black raft
of common scoters craft a disappearing act as they dive deeply in
great numbers then out of the blue they're back,

I head for the final tunnel suddenly fleet of foot emerging down in a dismal mizzle to the town of Saundersfoot, home of William Frost and the first wind tossed powered flight of eighteen ninety three sadly to his cost all his records were lost now buried in history, as I trot along the wide path I spot the harbour on the southern side where shipping would have tied up stranded on low tide awaiting the ensuing flood with coal or pig iron loaded on them, I stroll through the town taking this opportunity to use the ATM; there'd been a mining community here since the fourteenth century or more however these days there's no sign of rail-stock or stevedore the dock is home to pleasure cruisers engaged in recreation, in summer sail and powerboat flood the bay a tourist destination, all is quieter now as the rain drips down, time to exhale, the visitors gone away there's barely a scattering of fishermen at the harbourage today,

I pass the harbour wall up an incline replacing the paving for mud over the 'Ladycave' anticline heading for Rhode Wood I think the last time I came here was way back in my childhood probably with some specific Orielton primary school objective, irrespective, whose to say, I reach the trees still introspective I've been absent from Pembrokeshire for many years, returning coaxingly for weddings or funerals in tears or colloquially visiting family, those I left behind, the growing years have left some corollary discharge on my mind,

this trail through scenic woodland is notoriously arduous the ups and downs on muddy ground is heavy and laborious the emerald canopies contrive to shield me from the rain the daylight breaking through makes me feel alive again, alert to glimpse red squirrels that still populate this wood preparing for winter's fruitless climate busily stockpiling food.

out of the thicket and around Monkstone Point there's a murky view,
of Hean Castle once medieval *'Hen Gastell'* now a private endue, up
the coast a silhouette of Tenby shrouded in low cloudy dew, way
down on the alluring expanse of Monkstone sand deserted but for
a seemingly forlorn woman training her disconcerted mutt and a
tittering cwtch of teenagers in overcoats whose presence float me
back to my wittering adolescence, and all that transpires on these
hidden beaches that harness us and trap us and conspire with
perihelion sunsets inspired by Dionysus and Bacchus when desire and
wistful gyres around soulful beach-fires become pyres to our volition

however the path up here is six inches of sludge, six inches deep from
cueing ranks along the banks of cautiously creeping sheep, down
another slippery slope to a tinkling clearwater stream then speedily
up from Lodge Valley before I run out of steam, above a golden
leeway delta once Stanley Baldwin's holiday shelter on Waterwinch
Bay I ingress to the road that leads to the sanctuary of urbanness
where I toiled away my college breaks 'til finally reaching maturity,
my first memory of Tenby is as a six year old on another merry school
outing snapped for the paper climbing on a museum cannon
mounting,

origin of Robert Recorde progenitor of the equals sign, a seaboard
medieval ward with fine five arched barbican gatehouse, St Mary's
church synonymous with Jasper and young Henry's infamous escape
to exile, the midway Palmerston fort on St Catherine's isle plus the
lifeboat slipway of the RNLI

with its noesis art gallery and museum the cosmopolitan centre of
Sir Benfro, provenance to novelist jockey Dick Francis, sound
conductor Grant Llewellyn, artist Nina Hamnett Queen of Bohemia,
the list goes on, profound players Kenneth Griffith and Clive Merrison
and people come here from all around, mostly on holiday visits some
eventually settling down,

locals who enjoy the beaches students come for employ from nearby
and abroad, some for historical features, caravans come to annoy
other motorists on the winding, lofty hedged roads, Gwen and
Augustus John were born here, Myfanwy Evans (Piper) as well, me
to work in the Giltar Hotel with Mairwen and Miguel a kitchen skivvy
like Orwell in Paris, I soaked up the culinary arris like a graduand,
where I sharpened my pencils on guests, caressed first love and
midnight on the sand.

2. Whiteout Tenby—Freshwater East

overcast but dryer on the second morning of my trek now confidently
performing I march along the deck of the two mile stretch of my legs
on south beach, over dunes and trails carpeted with sea buckthorn to
reach the oldest golf course in Wales I peg inward and impeach on
Penally the probable or proverbial birthplace of St Teilo, I tally along
the rail track by St Deiniol's healing well whose holy waters, legends
tell, he delivered for lord and man all the way from the river Jordan,
on then to the abbey where in thirteen hundred and one the nuns of
Aconbury were granted the advowson, a mile inland is Gumfreston
Farm, where Helen Lewis hexed some sows that aborted their litter,
curiously during the bitter dunking fling when the 'witches hammer'
was in full swing no *dyn hysbys neu wrach* in Pembrokeshire were
ever incarcerated or put to the wrack

unavowed I run on to the Giltar Point high lands, close to cormorant
strewn St Margaret's and Caldey Islands once the vagrant rampart of
pirates Henry Morgan and Black Bart now where trappist monks
incant their adorations and brew fragrant scents, luckily permitted I
hurry past the rifle range drifts and history drenched remnants of
training trenches where young men prepared for the western front,

the coast path predestined confronts appealing coves and limestone
cliffs a hazy view of the perfect crescent shaped rift of sands and
dunes of Lydstep shoreline the saddle and ridge of Whitesheet Rock,
I hurry past the old limestone quarry a pock race inland is the Old
Palace or Lis Castle once a regal power, the court it's said of fifth
century prince of Dyfed Aergol Llawhir reportedly the father of Pwll, I
stalk past the groves as depressant draped clouds engulf the scenery
avoiding the cliff top walk where the yellow kidney vetch grows I spot
a distinctive red billed chough and a handful of crows,

beyond Skomar and down the steps to a more curious display, an uncarved dossal free arch the monumental 'church doors' at Skrinkle Bay where sea snail gastropod fossils lay, I rest with a coffee and a whiff of amphora, a favourite cove of my sister's, fulmars settle on the colossal cliffs of this abandoned cosy alcove unaware as yet of the peregrine falcon gliding effortlessly above, back up the stepped elevation I stroll round the old cold war thunderbird missile station now just a cracked concrete plinth formation, patched with grass and rust thankfully turning to dust F.A.B... yet lamentably with events in the Ukraine we just might need them again..*Het! (отказ),* I set on by Skrinkle Haven painted by Pre-Raphaelite John Brett, then a scamp along the path a bit edging the army camp to Conigar Pit,

just off Presipe in a December tempest of nineteen twenty nine was a vespertine scene, a modernist emulation to compare with Turner's 'Fighting Temeraire' a tug lugging the destroyer HMS Tormentor to the breakers yard, the whole aspect was marred when wretchedly both vessels ill-starred were lost in a furious sea storm bombard,

down at Coomb and around Rooks Cave the conglomerate behaves like sharpened spikes, a giant's hair brush jutting like pikes from the deep green sea bed, I'm surprised to see llamas grazing in the mist out of place in a field above Welsh cliffs, this drama, this whiteout echoes the fog that fell as the Mabinogion tells of the enchantment of Dyfed when the population vanished save for Pryderi and Rhiannon, Cygfa and Manawyddan, at Parson's Nose as clouds start to lift I follow the escarpments' shift turning in to 'King's Quoit' a neolithic cromlech on Manorbier point, taking in its littoral features humming the haunting tune by the Manic Street Preachers into Manorbier the firth of smuggler Captain Jack Furze and the picturesque stockade home of *Geraldus Cambrensis* chronicler of historic tales and his journey through Wales on his recruitment campaign for the third crusade, my gait quickens up the trail to East Moore cliff on to pretty Swanlake Bay over hilly heath through a West Moore spindrift arriving at the sandbanks of Freshwater East unable to outflank an arriviste peddler with a prosaic line of gab I assume he's here for the clinic and rehab

I escape past a corral of ponies where chiffchaff and wagtail bob in the scrub, the sporadic residence of another 'crazy chick' I reach my destination and head for the pub. we'd stop here on the way to West Trewent visiting my relations homestead and spent some time cowardly and craven with those rankle, spiting, ankle biting corgis my auntie bred, I had my first burger here a stomatic revelation, a mile up the road is Lamphey and the ruins of Bishop's Palace once used by members of the consistory, diocesans seeking solace, and where I delivered groceries with the doyen that was Bill when I spent a summer recess with Bronwen on Bethesda hill,

3. Bionomic Thrum Freshwater East—Freshwater West

resuming the tour under a cerulean blue sky, the vista is fresh like wearing glasses the first time a chromatic aberration scanning this visual mesh of sea, rock, sky and grasses, I climb the path to Trewent Point to view the plateau of Stackpole Head three miles in front, dotted pillow clouds above my head, shimmering sunlight and blue flicker like a gypsy queen gala shining through the natural arches of Greenala,

below the stimulating iron age hill fort of the Demetae, on to the asymmetrical syncline islet just off Stackpole quay where I stop for tea at the Boathouse as a group of divers arrive, the site of J D Innes pastel coloured coastline derive, a mile inland is the home of 'the dancing stones' and the set for David Tress' ogive action painting render of the church at Stackpole Elidor, I contrive to rest for five on a wooden seat

then pursue the path dotted with more folk I hoped I wouldn't meet, the weather changes everything here, I descend through the stone archway then fifty feet of surfeit steps to the celebrated Barafundle Bay, mitigating stumbling on the flowing dissipating sandpits, a bumbler as gorky's zygotic mynci would have it, traversing over the natural arches of Griffith Lorts Hole along the coastline towards Stackpole Head with its blowholes tunnels and caves, the going is relaxed and hearty with wide grassy trail manicured and shaven past Sandy Pit around Saddle Point down to where Church Rock marks the mouth of the beautiful bay at Broad Haven south,

the sandy beach I painted for Artie Williams, me and Paula picked small stones here, a trophy, a bit arty, well I am, more dunes to Bosherston lily ponds, in the shade I saw otters, a chantilly blonde not the lady brandishing excalibur, in the lazy summer heat of seventy six, betwixt horsefly and midge fishing pike under the eight arches bridge, back over the bunkers, target tramways and observation dugouts at Trevallen Downs to St Govan's Chapel and descending down the steps I grapple, counting as I go is a bit of a chore they never add up I've tried it before, set upon by pirates St Govan or Gawain hid in a cave, his silver bell of perfect tone was stolen, legend says saved by angels or fairies who encased it in stone, back up the steps in the wake and penetrating sone of aggravated gulls and kittiwakes, then on to Bosherston Head and the innate geo Huntsman's Leap, the phantasm of the mounted hunter who jumped the steep chasm; it wasn't the rock but a post hoc spasm of shock that slew him, I thread past the blowholes of Bosherston Mere where *'there is nothing to hope and nothing to fear'* then tread from Devils Barn Arch to the radar station at Saddle Head,

I recall a bruising parade tramp here as a *lancepesade* rank cadet and drove a centurion tank round Merion Camp, cruising pervade the amber counterpoint limestone outcrop at Newton Point on past a second radar mast and isoclinal piedmont spout of The Castle, another wave forged arch before a shorter march to Mewsford Point's aspect of the shore, clay and triassic gash-breccia of Bullslaughter Bay, a quick-time dash, check by those prime iron age forts at Mood Nose and Flimstone Bay with its scattered stacks and hard-severe climbs

on to the elegant impact of Elegug Stacks and a short trail to the archetypal Green Bridge of Wales scanning along this fine postcard coastline, the picton blue sky echoed on an almost ruffle free lapis sea towards Linney Head and not a merman in sight Henry, ferally aware of the utmost sinister menace hidden there notated by the distressing boast of ghostly shipwrecked lagan concealed beneath its hosting fenestral sends a shiver down my spine,

in sardonic revere mode I reverse back to the road it's a three mile
camber to Castlemartin scrambling around the firing ranges the
tarmacs tiring changes test my knees and my feet are throbbing I
pace another two and arrive at Freshwater West, the space Dobby
thought was *such a beautiful place* there he died and was laid to
rest, and where Robin Hood defeated the French? ...Hollywood!

the extended view from the top of the hill is a stunning array of
breakers and surfing spill, a spot I expended many youthful days
correlating the scenic sands and bionomic thrum from the car with
dad and mum relating stories of gathering purple green gelatinous
membranous seaweed strands to dry for making delicious lava bread
in the hut that still stands, fun days skipping over the banks on
Sunday afternoons years later motorcross on the upper dunes
swathed in prickly marram grass, with mates surfing and swimming,
stalking sticklebacks and eels over fahlband aggregates in the
estuary, for now though that's the end of my walk until January.

4. Walking Home Freshwater West—Kilpaison Bay

the festival season abrogated I resume my quest after a three month breach, on a hazy morning from Freshwater West beach, the corrugated ocean awaiting the wet-suited dawn patrol eagerly unzipping surfboards on the sand, sun and surf on the rise my climb outstripping both I turn as they reach the water's edge, gazing down from the hedge above Gravel Bay through the lazy dawning soft cumulus, yet the sky aloft is cyan blue crisscrossed with ribboned trails of muzzy early flights,

my breath visible and rasping in the chill, I achieve the dizzy curly heights by Black Cave gasping at the bucolic sight along the grasping coast, just as I get into my stride a gaping boast of path in front about eight feet wide has collapsed the red sandstone given way and almost gone I ramble on up the hill ghost around the heather pick my way hither and thither through gorse and bramble, making a forced mad scramble hell for leather through a blackthorn thicket, I transport myself piecemeal past East Pickard adjacent to the iron age fort to West Pickard catching a fox out in the open field, the last time that occurred was when Eric and I were hunting rabbits in a Narberth weald personating Pwyll and Arawn, Gweneira in her gauche said he's worse, I must perpend finding the courage and moral verve to visit my old friend

I amble down the snaky deep to a trickling stream again aware I must scale the sheer greasy steep on the opposite plane, flagging and parched, stopping to rest against a rebuttal pole before I reach the apical and spectacle of the natural geological arch at Guttle hole I stop for a stimulating coffee under the awn of a world war two pillbox I take a gander at the scenery then wander around a cavernous vesicle zawn.

15

carrying on to Parsonquarry Bay for the best view of Sheep Island, over another hill fort at Whitedole I lay eyes on South Studdock farm, where I first visited some cousins as a child on a family liaison in sixty one, still able to recall a gaslit supper of cheese and cawl (Welsh stew) on a long mahogany table such memories are few,

down on Castle Bay there's perfect examples of differential erosion, the view of Rat island and the ample round concrete formations of world war two gun port placements, on from here a precarious location the remnants of East Blockhouse fortification built on the orders of Henry VIII in fifteen thirty nine against the faith and threat of invasion by the Spanish and French nations, I round Lowrey's Rock which conveys me into the Haven and West Angle Bay

historical, here in 1405 a French army landed to fight Bolingbroke to the Glyndwr standard, analytical, you can find *Asterina phylactica*, small green starfish in gigapan pools but whimsical this is where I learnt fools play my first sandy beach jumping off rocks in the bay, sabbatical school day summers working on the hay, magical playing football against Merrion Camp Germans on boxing day, truly fun in the sun-strobe and a beer in the Globe, teenage years with Karen my first wife to be on a country bus, mother of my three children philosophical, she's no longer with us

still I put my thoughts behind me winding my way up the hill passed West Pill Farm until I'm a stone's throw from Thorn Island with its illustrious fort resistant to a Napoleonic storm, three thousand bulky ships have floundered or run aground along this risky coast's brisk sea, including most legendary the 'Loch Shiel' sunk in the eighteen nineties torn asunder off the Thorn with its seven thousand cases of whiskey whose disappearance remains a mystery, small wonder

as I ponder this tragedy and things I'm watching a staunch fire tug
exercising its pumps akin to a seagull stretching its wings preparing
to launch, I cavort by the Victorian defences of Chapel Bay Fort with
those 18" cannons then a short cant to the important and busy
lifeboat station, on around North Hill head to the 'Point House'
salutation where I stop outside for a swig of 'celtic pride' clocking
the anglers with their lugworm dig, I've been stranded here on high
tide, the ashen sky blue is replaced by a late afternoon miasma, at
rest the chill sets in I put on my bag zip up everything and pace the
shale and grit path along the 'Ridge' into Angle village

St Mary's graveyard
lie seven Japanese of
'Hirano Maru'

out beyond boats and ships a forest of mainsail and sprit then hills of
lobster baskets, I hasten away onto the strip I'm headed for Kilpaison
Bay, stifling my wits to the drone of images, keeping memories at bay,
for now I really am walking home, through brome fields, after that
I follow the low lying format and sallow cove of aragonite mudflats,
up ahead are the groundwork remnants of the BP pumping station,
now my homing instinct is the only navigational requisite so I turn my
attention to the godwits, sandpipers and curlews that inhabit the
shoreline and lava black rocks on this turbidite coastal plain with the
brackish marsh behind, this view, about face to Angle, from a field
chopping mangles on Hoplass farm, came the impulse for 'cofio' by
poet Waldo, like him rumination and reflection now commandeers
my mind,

for just up there in that hedgerow, we chopped down a trunk, logged it and lumbered it home in the snow, this shallow pond served as an ice rink, so numbered this anamnesis I think they'd take an essay to list, like family cockling days, in summer we'd stray just to swim and play in a tiny sandy bay all day, a whilom, stuffed in a canoe here with my older brother Haydn and friends I almost met my end when it upended I was wedged in it only to be dredged out at the very last minute, I trudged driven, unforgiven along this shore as a pubescent youth when plans went awry, my spiritual guarantor,

as a matter of fact half a mile tract inland across the flatter fields is Rhoscrowther where St Decuman was born, thought to be at the ex-Perrott's Eastington Hall, or Jestynton, home of Jestyn, Howel Ddâ Prince of Deheubarth's grandson, and where I grew up, once a busy tractored village with kids in the streets of Pleasant View and St Degmans, cricket, football and rugby on the green, children chasing tadpoles in the stream, Mrs Thomas and Matthias's petunias, begonia shrubs and daffodilled gardens the chestnut vicarage and youth club, pinnied and head scarfed mothers, four-eyes and lallydoggy nags Sunday school drags to Wallaston chapel, school bags and scallywags waiting for the bus, but just a handful of houses linger on after a shattering, clattering explosion at the refinery when a cracking tower blew up, most of the battered community scattered in waves, I pay my respects at my parents, brother's and uncle's graves

5. Genuflect Skeletons Kilpaison Bay—Pembroke Dock

under a weak veil of cloud I reboot my trip from Sawdern Point which
seems to impute on its tip a permanent cormorant, then on to
Palmerston's folly the mid nineteenth century fort at Popton, there's
a funny domestic report that my brothers Morris and Haydn sort to
sell my sister Blodwen here during post war operations, where I
delivered milk after school for the merchant navy congregation,
looking out over the river the vista is one of industrial corporations,
giant oil and gas tankers, huge refineries both sides of the haven,
ferries, fishing boats and power station. Lord Nelson, visiting the
harbour with the Hamiltons, described it as "the finest port in
Christendom"

blazing faster flanking the jetty over grazing pasture, reports relay the
fatted calf is getting too fat; Haydn in his heyday won a prize for
ploughing they say that's now old hat the purpose is not to disturb
the surface farming's altered out of all caveat, that's why the
yellowhammers are leaving and won't be coming back, on through a
defoliated pedunculate oak corridor partly cloaked in choking hedera
ivy delineated with nettle, fern and dock leaf, soaking up the
fimbriated atmosphere skirting the crude refining plant, pell-mell
down to the distinctive red ochre pebbled beach at Bullwell which
left me glued aligning scant visions of earlier places before the heavy
industry, the ruins of a cottage repatriates me with forgotten faces

let me explain I have retained an arcane childhood muse walking
with dad again from the village, we use the main road passed cherry
trees to a cousin's domain at Glebe Cross where honeysuckle backed
the old milk stand half covered in moss, we volplane down the lane to
the cottage and I play in the bay, my sisters say they also came, to
visit Christine and Jane, now long forsaken there was a wherry from
here to Hakin,

I continue onward and steadily upwards over a dead leaf carpet that creates a broad stabilizing surface over the gley soil floor, through a clearing I can see forward to Hobbs Point in the distance where we'd board the Cleddau King or Queen for ferriage from Pembroke Dock to Neyland before the opening of the bridge I leave the trees behind heading into open ground, up a steep sloping lane through the torrent of last night's teeming rainstorm running down to greet me, then a very gentle canter down the mayweed track to the environmental centre on Pwllchrochan flats, I proceed along the slatted boardwalk lead through the shoulder high reeds to St Mary's church, where my uncle Jack was interned in nineteen seventy three, where also lays historical novelist Emma Leslie

anyhow on and up past the old primary where my older siblings were schooled, at West Pennar was the dairy where I learnt how to milk cows, the farm's no longer here, back in around the power station the place I began my career discovering a wider world and knowhow, then over a slough and mud covered bridge, across the fields following the brow of a high fenced ridge around the sodden ploughed ground to Lambeth Farm which seems to have somehow become a shelter for old horses and ponies, the proud round castle walls hog the scene up Pembroke river as far as my eyesight allows

the journey now winds me to a small copse and the sun finally crashes through, light beams falling, scything the trees lighting up all the honey dew, olive and lime, the pistachio, mint and pine, the amber and fawn of this fallen foliaged avenue, even the blackbird calls its due, stepping stones over the inlet of Goldborough Pill, past the old limekiln to the road, round a pool half a mile up the hill near Hundleton where my great grandparents rest, is Orielton school

although sometimes silly sometimes tough the knowledge I left with,
subsuming *'Seagull Billy'* and *'Near Enough is not Good Enough'*
channelled my portfolio for the rest of my life, the headmaster's diary
has a nineteen fifty nine entry stating how 'there's a suspected case
of polio in a Rhoscrowther Family', that was me,

tracking down to Brownslate along the intertidal plate to West Grove
I open my gait passed Bentlass where the fated ferry to Pennar went
down in eighteen eighty nine, drowning master, mate and passengers
past Fleet Farm then from the gate down a lane to Quoits Mill at the
foot of the bluebell wood on Bowett hill, straight on to Monkton,
where I lived in the late seventies for a three year spate, Eric lodged
with us here awhile, oh he's refusing to medicate, there's a first rate
neolithic cave by the river, the church here was reinstated on the
ruins of a priory circa ten ninety eight and has a host of pulsating
tales, like the genuflect skeleton speculated to be that of a nun
hidden in an edifice, naturally there's a ghost, just prate,

legend tells of a concealed subterranean passage to the castle they
can't locate the entrance, where Cromwell mounted his cannon to
assail it in sixteen forty eight, down the inclined Awkward Hill past
the wall of the fourteenth century Old Hall, on over Monkton Bridge
and around the profound, picturesque, renowned, even domineering
William Marshall's Pembroke Castle of course the birthplace of the
crowned King Henry VII founder of the Tudor dynasty, once the UK
site for the Templar Knights and the easel for many other tales that
abound including Nest and a weasel, as a child it's where we held
outstanding summer fetes, which felt closer to its history than any re-
enactment or model can relate, famously painted during the
Romantic era by Richard Wilson and JMW Turner, where Anthony
Hopkins played his part as a fledgling Richard the Lionheart

the medieval walled compound of Pembroke, Cromwell quartered in
the York Tavern during his pounding two month siege, home to
composer Daniel Jones, Welsh rugby liege Jonathan Thomas and a
quarter of gzm, in seventeen twenty five Daniel Defoe pronounced
'the largest and richest most flourishing town in South Wales', DT's
'Pembroke city' well that's changed, as has my hometown memories
of the October fairground, Lane's sweetshop, Haggar's Cinema, Hill's
newsagent, Brown's cafe and where I got my haircut

on the Mill Pond the usual wedge of swans and a couple of coots are
there, If you stand and stare you may clamp eyes on super-tramp's
kingfisher, I cross Mill Bridge once part of an old mill sifting wheat
and corn, at the Green up the hill was 'Riverside' maternity hospital
where I was born, passing houses on the ridge that one time held
French captives, until released by local lasses, back westward passes
the effusive dam and sluice, I tarry along the opposite bank goose by
the quarry that borders Pembroke school, sports centre and hospice,
where I, *gratis dictum*, escaped to play squash and tennis,

on up to Pennar where they once farmed oysters, in the late
nineteenth century there were billets for submarine mine stores,
torpedo missile testing took place along these shores, I chock down
to Pembroke Dock on Commercial Road next to the neat, textbook
mid nineteenth century Martello Tower on Front Street, where I
learnt to water ski, it's here I complete my tour for today

once Paterchurch now Pembroke Dock, where my paternal
grandparents lay and I was educated went to youth club my rugby
cultivated, home to the Irish ferry terminal for many years an
energetic military municipal haunt of a Royal Naval yard two hundred
and sixty three vessels launched one marred cursed by Betty Foggy,
gunboats, battleships and almost forgot three Victoria 'n' Albert royal
yachts plus Han Solo's 'Millennium Falcon' put together in a hanger
built for Sunderlands the last one seen off to Hendon by Hughie
Green, the dock was heavily bombed in nineteen forty one

6. Towns and Industry Pembroke Dock—Sandy Haven

a St David's Day early resumption crossing the Cleddau bridge
conjunction under a melancholy eclipse, remembering its thunderous
collapse during construction, up stream after Lawrenny where the
Creswell river junction runs it's course to the flavoursome casked
beer of the Cresselly Arms, the river splits, I fished the eastern section
with Eric, one morning we encountered a romp of otters, the stout
procession robbing us of our *bridyll* or trout consumption,

down river already tugs and boats have no compunction a propos
disturbing the gentle waters and me recalling teenage fornication
near here in Honeyborough Green frenzied pencil lines and tempera
dreams, walking over Westfield Pill the marina's growing still, I slide
down an oak lined sodden ramp a field of shires nod and stamp
signifying my passing expecting a formal introduction the pathside is
littered with discarded intoxication contamination and takeaway
defecation which grant the area a depressed manifestation, if only
the sun would shine

Neyland the 'yacht haven' and birthplace of 'Affinity' author award
winning novelist Sarah Waters, the town grew around a railway
terminus with a busy steamship service to Cork and as far away as
Brazil, the bustling of ship and wherry, ice factory folk and fish
market skill, the immense lattice of rail tracks, tense, bustling with
merry working stock to and fro on the ferry from Pembroke Dock all
long gone, a statue, erected to the towns founder was stolen
presumably to melt down as it's hard and irksome to sell a large
bronze image of Isambard Kingdom Brunel, but it was soon replaced

the besmirched skies impel me on along Church Road passed
Llanstadwell to St Tudwal's church its hallowed appellation refers to
a sixth century monk, coalition founder saint of Brittany, vessel of
the dragon symbol of Tregor, this next phase takes the form of a
privet hedged moor I laze on a bench and gaze across through the
anti-meridiem haze to East and West Pennar at the Pembroke River
cleft, I raise myself and resume my quest

the coarse path leads to Hazelbeach past shipping containers over a
reinforced iron grated road bridge using all my resource through the
square tin tunnel like an army assault course threading with poise
past the gorse lined refinery fence to the vehicular hoys by the
perpendicular pier at Newton Noyes, one time home to a US
military force and Royal Navy ammunition depot, heading north to
meet the road into Milford Haven town via the Black Bridge I follow
the footpath down to the view from the concourse on the 'Rath'
where I take a pew by the dextrorse fisherman statue

Milford from Meirfjordr a Scandinavian name locale to the Torch,
the Waterfront Gallery and Paper Aeroplanes from where Henry II
began his Irish campaign, a church was dedicated to Thomas a
Becket, in Shakespeare's 'Cymbeline' play a subset, the town we
severalize was established by chance by Sir William Hamilton from
his wife's inheritance realized as a grid planned as a whaling station
for which arrived quakers from a Nantucket location, a Naval
dockyard and shipbuilding came but fishing's what lasted and
symbolized its fame.

I knuckle down and buckle up my ramshackle pack retake the track
with aching back a stoical haemagogue jog along to the road
loosening my joints past the catalogue of yachting marina masts
down to the typical dock where fishing smacks berth on which my
eldest brother Morris worked, a bestirred flock of gulls circle,
undeterred I rub my calves pull up my socks, up the hill that way was
once the royalist Pill Fort built on the 'Gunkle' an assail by four
parliamentary ships resulted in a diabolical surrender in a day

but I cross the bridge between Hakin and Hubbardston where I
pursue a way back to the path on to Gelliswick Bay to join curlew and
Pioden yr môr on the limpet and barnacled shore in my youth there
was an equivocal cull as a last resort, due to the undue critical full of
cockles they extort, smaller fishing tubs jolly away from the yachting
club slipway, pollock, bass, bream, smooth-hound and ray are caught,
there's a rear view pane of a further Palmerston's folly Hubbardston
Fort once manned by the regiment 24th of foot of 'Zulu' fame

over one pipeline under the other, the last jetty finally ends the
scramble and hullabaloo of towns and industry, then a disport
amble to South Hook and the purlieu Hook Fort, part of the same
royal commission designed by Gordon of Khartoum, was crewed by
a WREN division in World War Two, flanking the bank of oil refinery
tanks I turn north to Kilroom Bay and spot a harsh lank track
meandering down through the broom to the sparse sandy plots
between the sandstone rocks dotted along its length and the oceanic
spume, to scary a climb for weary limbs,

a lane along at Muns Mouth steers me on to Herbrandson's modest
church St Marys, it has the kudos of a rare reredosse a celebratory
thank you for the miraculous safe return of all parish sons, not one
lost conversely to the rank doom of world war one!

back on the coast path in the now dank gloom a house light beckons
I groom my way across the stepping stoned stream in Sandy Haven
where Henry I's Flemish settlers would land a favourite haunt of
Graham Sutherland, the burial place following Gwalchmai's betrayal,
the bay where blue jays scream their play in the moss wrapped plume
of trees that loom along the claybank above the long abandoned
limekiln, at the end of the day as the chill threatens

7. Transformative Vortex Sandy Haven—St Anne's Head

I start this morning with an epiphany per se some circumspection, the sun is bright early the sky has a tiffany blue complexion, the problem with ending each walking day at a bay is you begin the next sectional foray with a hill not perfection still I'm up by an additional iron age bastion cadaver at Little Castle Head I notice a divergent distraction of a golden section back in the direction of the haven shrouded in advection fog a silhouette of the Stack Rock stronghold, on reflection the scene is reminiscent of some old seadog fiction of vanishing islands not to mention the *tylwyth teg or dynon bach teg* inhabiting them who frequented Milford market, on inspection the atoll would evaporate so the myth imparted perhaps 'The Dyfed Triangle' or another dimension?

I chance it darker past the transit marker mast suddenly overcast, around Butts Bay the clouds clear away fast, at Chester Point I cast an eye on the silurian igneous, mudstone and sandstone contrast of Longoar Bay over the blackthorn bushes and then away to Great Castle Head, where I felt a drip, which was not in the forecast hopefully just a blip, half of this celtic fort alas was lost to landslip beyond the shipping monitoring radar station after Gray Rocks is the little sandy haven of Lindsway, where prone palynomorphs foil neat evince marls in the silurian gray stone, this was the first Welsh soil to greet Prince Charles, my champion Prince of Wales who still sixty years on anticipates the throne

next door at Longberry Bay the Donna Marika conveying eleven thousand tons of aviation fuel ran aground all were brave all behaved no one panicked ship, crew and contents were saved, a natural aperture at Watch House Point points to Monk Haven formerly the landing site for pilgrims to St David's from here up a lane less than a mile hails to St Ishmaels which was a principle diocese or cantref of Rhos spanning the late seventh century reign of Rhein ap Cadwgan regaining the shale broads around a squally disused lime quarry into Dale Roads past Musselwick Bay's black shales and red sandstone rock face, at the Gann there's a trail for high tide crossing over Mullock Bridge, legend tells this is where Rhys ap Thomas stood under as the Earl of Richmond traversed over to observe the advice of the Bishop of St David's to absolve Rhys of his obligation and word to Richard III

anyway it's low water so I take the stepping stones over the saltmarsh as the sky clears, the weather, I cavil about it every afternoon, along Pickleridge adjacent to the gravel pit quarry lagoons that attract so much wildlife, today there's whimbrel, an egret and finches festoon the vale suitably atmospheric traversing into Dale I find myself in ersatz conversation with Eric? shipping limestone, coal and culm once a hectic port, the best place in Wales to find the sun perfect for picnics for boating class curriculum au fait with kellick and sails

thirteenth century Dale Castle once the regale of Robertus de Vale, from his granddaughters hailed Owain Glyndwr and Henry Tudor later gained by Lucy Walters' family she the mistress of Charles II, he died heirless and his papist brother James II obtained the throne, their ill-stated feudist son the Duke of Monmouth was executed after an ill-fated protestant rebellion

I take the tarmac path and photograph some wood-sculpture cenotaph on the hill, a real muddy venture through Blue Anchor woods where I hear the tapping of a woodpecker or could it be the 'tolaeth', on to Dale fort which was once a further Victorian citadel now a field studies centre I imbricate the thicket and Castlebeach Bay then on to Watwick where the trawler *Shore Breeze* beached in the thirties, one brave crewman's endeavour to scale the inured cliff face was overcome by exposure no others endured, its brutal how something so full of living can be so wholly unforgiving, I tramp on to West Blockhouse fort once Henry VIII's creation, then a Palmerston fixation now a stunning holiday location

yet I'm buoyant veering east again, down into the unassuming least
flamboyant Mill Bay it's enclosed and easy to imagine the drama the
arrant clamour of bassinet and red dragon banner, even if a fraction
of his faction of fifty five ships disembarked at Dale, a transforming
rive in our history, the dearth concealed landing in fourteen eighty
five of Henry Tudor on his way to Bosworth field

as I ascend the gradient now at the apex on the aperture of the
Haven I painfully ruminate another transformative vortex of a very
different nature; the distressing grounding of the *Sea Empress*
causing tens of thousands of tonnes of crude oil to spew out of hand
confounding and devastating the delicate ecology of the coast and
the islands... distracted I arrive at the lighthouse on St Anne's Head
with abstracted memories of a school expedition that said I do
remember well the enjoyment of subsequent assignments which
erupted from that excursion and here I go again struggling with
cynghanedd ac awdl, out there looking west a war grave lies beneath
those shadowy waves in the guise of two landing crafts that perished
in a gale during a wartime exercise, enough for today

the summer found me clutching a commemorable vesperal
back in Narbeth in thoughtful visceral sombre at Eric's funeral

8. *Homo Sapien Accommodation*
St Anne's Head-Martin's Haven

it's early December when I restart my walk traversing north from St
Ann's towards Frenchman's Bay the predominant colours are mauves
and greys, sky, rocks and sea, deep green grass and bush the usual
lush yellow gorse and vetch the pink campion are nowhere to be seen
along this stretch there's some white streaks of cloud and foam,
inland even overcast as it is there's still a view of Skokholm Island
where the earliest bird observatory in Britain was planned by Ronald
Lockley the first person to gain an Oscar for a nature documentary,
there you'll find large colonies of manx shearwaters, storm petrels
and puffins in the seas harbour porpoise, grey seals and risso's
dolphins not to mention an abundance of flora and fauna

I'm passively walking pagan's paths skirting the iron-age mound
around Little Castle, it's fascinating to contemplate a familiar
perspicacity three thousand years earlier, I spot a kestrel secreted on
a clifftop ledge actively stalking pigeons, at Long Point looking east
over the cove at Dale Castle where cattle are boarding for market,
increasing my gait back up the hill, gratefully watching a graceful
waterfall display beside the lodge above sandy Westdale as it
meanders and glides down the bay, I stop for coffee on a super
standpoint by the disused airfield at Hooper's Point down below in
forty one the *'Faraday'* was laying some cables when she was
accosted by enemy planes, a third of the crew were lost, with an ad
hoc stare across the grey unstable sea I spy the ferry from Roslaire on
its uneasy queasy crossing to Pembroke Dock

at the considerable span of Marloes Sand with it's hard aeronion, sheinwoodian and homerian 'chimneys' a favourite spot for budding Louis and Mary Leakeys with testament of life's first trot on dry land, there's just the solitary figure of a walking man, peaceful but for cormorants on the rocks and the ubiquitous gulls that gather and flock this desolate view countermands recently shot foreboding illusionary peaky surrounds from 'snow white and the huntsman' or distant sites of 'lions in winter' fights, at the beach's north bound stands the mat flat plateau of Gateholm Island it has a low tide access along 'Albion Sands' branded by the visible ruin of the damned paddle steamer sent aground pursuing the perilous short cut thru Jack Sounds

among the malm rock of Watery Bay rath a purport foretime scene of another hill fort, excavated by 'The Time Team' along with settlements on Gateholm, a sublime halfback break to Victoria Bay finds me flanking a field of prime Welsh Black steak as served at the Old King's Arms, even stood bravura in front of me I've no qualms about devouring it, perusing a relatively calm Jack Sound in bygone day's livestock was ferried athwart in a praam, nowadays they ride these rapids in kayaks for fun

round to Little Castle Bay's balmy view of Grassholm Island six miles out through Broad Sound with its alarming voluble gannetry, or 'Gwales' as stated in the white book tales of the decapitated head of Bran and for eighty years a haven for Pryderi and Manawyddan, then there's Rainy Rock replicating an arm pointing out the islands, a short reach inland to heartily greet Marloes Mere, leeches from here were used on Harley Street, I pass Mouse Haven to the less calming Pitting Gales Point and the disarming Bench Islands, at the fascinating talus beach of Deadman's Bay Ray Howard-Jones eked its colours onto her vacillating canvas when she rented a reticent cottage nearby,

without delay I power on, past Lockley Lodge Visitors Centre and
the celtic carved stone in the wall that once enclosed the deerless
deer park and the largest iron age hamlet, concluding another
day's strut at the coastguard's hut at Martin's Haven,

I escorted Paula here in the pollen colic heat of summer to apprise
her with seals and pups I surmise there were at least forty auroral
sightseers; however these days this time of year's solitary
melancholic beat of glummer timbre appeals and cups to my guise,
bisecting here and Midland Isle there's a plethora of wrecks that
strayed on an intersect course of cause and effect like the 'Lucy' when
Cable Rock sprung her decks on Valentine's Day, the 'SS Moseley'
defrayed by The Neck subject of the very first BBC S.O.S. direct
appeal

traversed by sea from the bay beyond Midland and The Neck is
Skomer the grandest of the island array, dispersed among the spec,
these lava spumed volcanic rocks contain half the world population
of manx shearwaters that trek to South American migrations so
even more affecting was a fatigued flock's collision with the power
station wall during a brouhaha squall in the stagflation years, as well
as puffins, petrels and guillemots an innate selection of *rodetia,
charadriiformes,* and *legomorpha* it has its own Skomer vole
myodes glareolus skomerensis plus *homo sapiens* accommodation

9. Modest Acumen Martin's Haven—Broad Haven

a new day pale blue sky zigzagged with broken flight trails and galloping marestail the sun still gagged delays behind the rocky crag as I head east by West Hook farm, in the region of High Point a freighter went down snagged lugging its sagging slate payload, East Hook farm is up the lane on my right with its prize bagging potatoes I well-nigh indite a georgic line striding along a short mud drag to Howney Stone at Hopgang the unmistakably languid flight of *barcud goch* a red kite glides by then steadily drifts out of sight, I duck down to light my pipe behind a trite gorse bush the wind is quickening, at the arenite Musselwick Sands with its ragtag black shale beneath red sandstone slag, then on to the aptly tagged Black Cliff

on passed the old quarry pit to the red stacks at Tower Point I orbit around Nab Head's iron age fort where a mesolithic virgin image and flint factory was found, then edging the steep geo Huntsman's Leap I trot past another fort on Castle Head tagging the perimeter wall I spot the flags of St Brides Castle

a mimesis really the stately home of the High Sherriff later on of the sixth Baron Kensington, in the nineteen twenties it became a sanatorium for tuberculosis patients now a classy holiday let, I lurch on by the old limekiln to the church rededicated by the classis to St Bridget, the original utilised as a fish factory as prophesised was swept to sea, and as portended ended the herring trade, only the graves remain, I carry on along the chocolate box bay, where the 'Ceffyl Dwr' once bore a dismayed farmer away to a watery end, St Brides is looking resplendent today, accounts for its name are vague I confess the telemetry that links Sain Ffraid to Ceridwen mother of Taliesin, goddess of poetry whose basis stem from the Gogynfeirdd achieves my modest acumen

I chant an epyllion excerpt climbing by Cliff Cottage, chock past The
Falls and the scant shingle Warey Bay over Halfway Rock which
looks like a pocked steak mallet, on to Mill Haven past the palate
limekiln and Alain Ayers sculpture 'womb of the sea' a tramp inland
is Broadmoor farm where you can 'glamp' in a Mongolian yurt, at
the anticline Foxes Hole a curt seam of coal was mined where the
rock faces transfer to grey igneous diocite then the platy mica schists
at Dutch Gin, I pass 'the walking eye' above Brandy Bay where a
chatty hiker sits and blocks the way, he ratifies unsurprisingly that
both coves where stalked by His Majesty's Revenues in years gone by,

another iron age promontory fort on Howney Stone rath, at Ticklas
Point there's guillemots and shags on the rocks, east of Holywell a
disused airfield used for Wellingtons hunting U-Boats during WWII
by a Czechoslovak garrison, I take a break at Borough Head looking
back at the cavity in Stack Rocks half a mile directly out to sea, in
gnathic comparison to a giants blackened lower incisors emerging
from the deep, as I peep east over Goultrop Roads red-throated
divers sweep by, out there wherever the Santa Cruz went down is
a cheap $2½ million in gold I'm told that's never been found,

I ponder the hush and majestic serenity of the scenery too plush
for embellish or eulogy, affecting my availability heuristic to imagine
violent murder yet that's what occurred here in the recent past,
suddenly it's a different world as I enter the sessile oak, beech and
pine woods the sun breach and fine raffish birdsong, a steep dash
flaying tall grass along the track down passed Sheep Wash Bay
where shepherds just fifty years back would flock before shearing, I
trek to Little Haven dock, over the Settlands steering down the pier
ending the day strolling along that flat golden beach casting a
long shadow in the fully bronzed and green flash afterglow, no not
a case for 'mulder and scully', to reach Broad Haven

Little Haven once a fishing and coal mining enterprise now the
'Havens Community' rely on leisurely pleasure seeking and
gourmandising aegis from their alluring eating places and easily
accessible beaches, my finest memories of Sunday School outing
pieties was ice cream and cricket on the sand here in the sunny day
cool swinging sixties,

10. A History Lesson Broad Haven—Newgale

Broad Haven beach doesn't look the same this morning, rather like a scene from storming nineteen thirties movie 'The Hurricane' well perhaps not quite such as no Dorothy Lamour in sight... shame, it's wild with grey loaded nimbus, crest strewn breakers and strong gusts, the Sleek Stone 'sofa's' not looking comfy, coal measures to Den's Door stack at leisure to the natural hogback arch of Haroldston Bridge a favourite coasteering ridge nobody's jumping off today, past Settling Nose I stray over the sloping Chins above the bay is the thin northern limit of variscan oregeny rock where spoils from mining toil mock the natural scree, over which is a soiree of cobs and ponies manes and tails flailing wildly on the stiff clifftop breeze matching the *ceffylau gwyn gwyllt* on the sea,

then down the graven gravel path to Druidston Haven's shore greenshank and sandpipers shelter amongst the crore dark shales by the mafic cubby hole caves, on this beach in seventeen ninety one HMS Increase had come undone not bearing rum or gems on her prow were drums of condemned gunpowder scavengers retreated from the explosive fright as hair and clothing were set alight, it's not an uncommon sight to see horses ridden along the inshore surf, back up the trochanteric tedium of steep arrant barred wooden steps a scrubby jounce to the sparse turf path turning to see the avant-garde grass covered atrium glass louvered proscenium of 'Malator' or locally 'telly tubby house',

in specie Druidston doesn't alight from druid but Drue a twelfth century knight, the sight at Priest Vault is one of heightened wave vivacity crashing foaming spew on the indurated rocks below, I'm virtually walking at right angle fighting to stay upright against the unbridled might of the wind as I find shelter at a hedge I'm directed at the ledge I step away...... from the edge,

then I bolt on passed the arches at North and Madoc's Havens and
down to the safe haven at Nolton, safe if you're fond at all of sports
like segway racing, even absorbing, if you wonder what it's like to be
a football maybe zorbing is your thing, I stop for coffee on the steps in
the bay, a sheltered space halfway up the north face screened by the
cliff, a hundred and fifty years back the hush now would have been
engulfed by the rush of smoke from packed steam trams and crush of
paddle steamers as coal was tracked from Trefrane Colliery to a
thrusting harbour,

I push on to the cave in Davy Williams Haven past the pebbled bay of
Roaring Cave then to the large peak stack of Rickets Head I wend by
the relics of the Trefrane mine engine shed and red brick chimney
the area's potmarked with disused shafts and stark quarries this
whole region marks the northern edge of the anthracite seam that
extends on a diagonal arc from here to Amroth, I press on by sea
froth crawling up the mudbank on an anabatic current, beyond the
recumbent blockwood bench at Maidenhall Point, along the sand
another redundant quarry near Sibbernock Point and a two mile
expanse of deserted Newgale sands in front of me

a history lesson, after nearly a two hundred year session of Welsh
Princely contention and Norman aggression Henry III's succession in
twelve sixteen and the cession of the barons domination, South
Pembrokeshire, *byth cael ei ailadrodd a byth eto,* yielded to Norman
suppression, a lineation delineated with a wanton procession of
castles stretching from Newgale to Amroth or for completion to
Laugharne, I can find no validation or vindication of design to follow
the northern collocation of the coalfield and mines, the partition
eternised as the 'Landsker Line' our own little "Schandmauer"

head lowered into the wind picturing the heat of Delirium's video
for 'Silence' a sultry couple free-running on a hyperthermic beach,
another Newgale scenario hypothermic promenading on Boxing
day, today's stormy milieu parallels the parable of the passing of St
Caradoc, the nuncio cast his casket and cargo on the shore as the
bearers sheltered from a downpour, they returned to find hereby
the sarcophagus was dry, a chapel was erected to commemorate the
miracle, finally attaining this vast lido I conclude today's itinerate at
the Duke of Edinburgh Inn in a vaguely guarded state, the original
was washed into the sea! at any rate I'll be back in January

11. Residuum Chattel
Newgale—St David's

during the bank holiday blanket rain and gales wreaked havoc along these shores Brandy Brook has burst it's banks and up here at Bryn-y-Mor it looks like the coast has been visited by the 'decepticon demolisher' as if the storm beach now on the vistaed road went thru' a stone polisher the event exposed a petrified woodland ten thousand years old, spectrometer specified,

high above today there's a cold blue sky washed in places by purple hazy grey vapour traces, out to sea it's calm but visibility is limited, mammy used to say 'you can't control the weather', I wonder if that's still true, gazing down at the sand thoughts of a fatal hand when a paragliding tragedy collided with the mound beneath my feet, a mile inland is Brawdy Cawder Barracks once an electronic warfare shield against cyber attacks before that a supersonic air force base on which I played isotonic rugby against a USAF company amidst the chronic din of jets taking off and landing, there was a Roman fort nearby at Castle Villa or Cas Wilia and the Scourfield production of Anne's abduction

passing the ordovician arch and dolerite dyke at Pwll March beside Cwm-Bach bay and it's rhyolite archway that you can only examine on low tide, past Ogof Felen outwash whitewashed by cormorants, across a high stream at Porthmynawyd to an iron age fort in amid the projection of Dinas Fach I then point my way in right on an inland trot to the Pointz Castle twelfth century motte once occupied by Poncé a Poitevin knight leaseholder by appointment to bishop Peter de Lera

I hie to the attractive bay of Ogof y Cae, in passed the spiralling
cataract on Stacen y Brenhin and the baluster arch at Aber Dwrain
around the Dinas Fawr peninsular where Germans mined silver in
the sixteenth century, at Pen Dinas I glance back at the crepuscular
rays along the bay the sun struggles to break out with little success,
on along the minor crests of Aber West while I look down on Porth y
Bŵch where in seventeen seventy three the 'Phoebe & Peggy' hit the
beach, as foragers snapped fingers to release their prized pickings
rescuers striving to save crewmen and passengers were swamped
and capsized, a sickening cost with a total loss of sixty lives,

from here the inland route to St Elvis Farm or St Aelbyw the sixth
century cleric who baptised St David at Porth Clais and his sacred well
where mediaeval folk took the waters then lay prone on the flagstone
of the nearby cromlech as they slept revitalization came but if the
white bird *Caladruis* loomed it brought ruinous doom and devastation

I retrace my paces to the coast at Porth Gwyn, grace by Carreg Dilys,
on Penrhyn I gaze down on Black Rock at the carapace mouth of the
slow paced river then glare out farther at the cambrian dacite Mare
and Scar islets, turning in past St Elvis Rock, down to unbrace at
Gwadn Bay such a gentle place to rest, where 'the Smalls' lighthouse
was erected, over the wooden bridge I race up past the iron age fort
along the Gribbon chase, on through the meagre woods above the
river, bearing down into the graceful rea past the historic limekilns
facing the galvanised bridge area of lower Solva

in the middle ages this was a major trading station later the now
port for emigration to New York, birthplace of Ysbryd Solva's Miec
Stevens and Spurs footballer Simon Davies, songster David Gray of
'*Babylon*' fame was raised here, Cedric Morris painted the town, it
has the oldest continued working Woollen Mill in the county, latest
edition, they've used the neighbourhood for a new rendition of
'Under Milk Wood' no webbed-foot cockle woman on view today or
grey wagtails I'm happy to say, Wales' first butterfly farm, and where
you might get pleasure from a duck race at Easter

winding my way up and out of the harbour about Careg Lyfn
overlooking Sterling Hock and the arch at Gweni, I chock past
Ystafelloedd to Segar Rock, below is Ogof Tobac and the alleged
tunnel that rambled to Llanunwas farm where the wrecking
scrambles were distributed by the Laugharnes, at the Cradle a
shocking faux pas the tugboat Vericos Alexia was towing two sister
tugs from Liverpool to Greece, bugs bared when her hawsers caffled
and all three where snaffled paying *Charon* on the rocks,

around Loch Warren to the lapidified leaf springs of Haccesh a path
swings north to Whitchurch the hometown of Adam Houghton
fourteenth century St David's bishop and Edward III's flag stop lord
chancellor, who later presided over the marriage of his grandson
Richard II and Anne of Bohemia, along by Aber Llong runs an eight
octave stream via Nine Wells quelling its falling knell into the bay,
past the iron age fort by the geo Porth y Rhew a geological arch and
issue of large peronopsis trilobite fossils, on the opposite axis is a
draught horse sight on Morfa Common harbouring a string of grey
and marron shires parading their breeding

I carry on to Ogof Mwn strolled to Carreg y Barcud, monoclonal over-
fold of jasper purple sandstone at Caer Bwdy Bay where the
cathedral grey stones came from, then blister on to the iron age fort
and fissure at Pleidiau Rock I spot a fishing boat flocked by gulls in
sandy Caerfi Bay out past the eco-farm's array of organic crops then
up the top and on around Pen y Cyfrwy to St Non's

residuum chattel of the medieval chapel rest vicinal to a celtic
communal complete with standing stones, a zenith deistic
assignment the anticlerical alignment it's not the liturgical east, site
of St David's devine creation from the violation of Non by Sanctus
Prince of Ceredigion, nearby is the newer 'chapel of our holy lady',
then the holy well whose waters were spent in apostolic bequeath
by his holiness pope Benedict XVI on his tour to British shores, then
there's the grandiose stone building of St Nons retreat, run by 'The
Sisters of Mercy' order of nuns I take the neat path on to the city
before I lose the aphelion sun another section done

St David's with a populace of 2K or less the smallest city in the UK,
address of the 'Oriel y Parc' Gallery, Wales footballer Ian Walsh and
geologist Henry Hicks FRS, where Gruffydd ab Einion discovered the
secret of the disappearing islands and the *'Plant Rhys Ddwfn'* I reach
the Cathedral in a late afternoon pall of purple stone reflected across
a cardinal sky, David's monastery stood on the site of the Bishops
Palace ruins, the constructs ransacked many times by marauding
Vikings pillaging and murdering several bishops, William the
Conqueror, Henry II and Edward Longshanks all gave thanks' at St
David's shrine, two pilgrimages here were equal to one devine trip
to Rome, the Cathedral structure and design begun in eleven twenty
three extended until the sixteenth century with enhancements
fashioned by Welsh architect John Nash on the crest of the
Enlightenment

12. Counting the Stars St David's—White Sands Bay

I balked my last planned walk, banned by a storm warning command to stay away from the coast and indeed such was the wind speed, wave-fetch and backwash the bus I caught from St David's was swept across Newgale sand the following day, catastrophic, half the strand at Amroth was washed away and prolific havoc wrought throughout the mainland, still a National Geographic pole unfurled this as the second most rated coastal park in the world

it's a drizzly opaque mid-March daybreak in a heliotrope fog of derisory ocular misery, defiling my binocular scrutiny of the landslip and natural arch of Porth Coch Mawr this specific spectacle of coastline is a dramatic display of baroque power and the frantic, upheaval elemental in it's formation, gently on to the popular coasteering venue of Chanter's Seat opposite the sheer steep composite slab of Trwyn Cynddeiriog in vogue with climbers along with the antilog 'Crack' on Porth Ffynnon,

I spin on past it's vertical strata portiére overhangs to Porth Clais the merchant logistic anchorage for St David's City prevalent 'til the late stage of the twentieth century, it's past includes ancient Roman masonry in the harbour wall, remnants of old limekilns and a salient gasworks once where the car park is, the site of infant David's lambent baptism and where the *Twrch Trwyth* landed on a trenchant rampage through South Wales with King Arthur, Gwyn ab Nudd and their pageants hot on the trail

from the harbour along the path overlooking Llech Cyllyll the
prospect encapsulated by Donald McIntyre in flat acrylics, then the
wave cut cryophilic raised beach bent by Ipswichian interglacial
melting ice shaping Ogof Golchfa or 'washing place cave', as I peruse
the atoll Halftide Rock a mile out I'm bemused by the waveless seas'
eristical calm, I turn then stroll on over the arch by Ogof Lle-sugn
stretching out beyond Precite Head the 'granophyres' white micro-
granite of silica, feldspar and mica intruded into the volcanic rocks
of the Treginnis Headland are the islets Careg Fran and Carreg yr
Esgob where little Johnny Ellis clung on for dear life all night long
through a pitiless tempest the sole survivor of the 'Susannah' when
it wrecked upon the rock,

I turn to the equally salic Porthlysgi Bay its eponym was the sixth
century Gaelic raider who beheaded Celtic chieftain Boia the last
druidic ruler of Pebidiog whose stronghold stood on the summit
of Clegyr Boia a mile inland, there's a little anecdote that his wife
Satrapa sent her maids to seduce David's followers and induce
them to disband, the mound immortalised in paint and print by
by Neo-Romantic Graham Sutherland as was much of the valley
around, passing Maen Llwydwyn I spot two sparse tree sparrows in
the harsh hawthorn brush, behind Porth Henllys bay flush to my right
is a small pool where a flock of lapwings floccule in aerobatic display I
scan back from Ogof Mrs Morgan bay at the gobsmack view of the
slot like arch in Careg yr Esgob

the rock formations here, *sine qua non*, are three ton and ninety
five million years old, on a southern diagonal from Newgale the
rock is a vernal one hundred and fifty million years younger, or in
that region, contemplating these timescales, cause me panic like
cogitating quantum mechanics or counting the stars, back on terra
firma humming a sort of canto as I round Ogof Cadno, on from Pen
Pedol I clock the little islet Shoe Rock then caught flight by Pen Dal-
aderyn the most westerly point on the coast,

on an utterly clear day along this coastpath every click of my
shutter emotes Barthes *'camera lucida'* yet here today surveying
this wild, wet and gloomy panorama the rock structures and
contiguous colours are eminently more wondrous, subtle and
vibrant and the solitude in which I've placed myself colludes, no
demands empathy in this *'gwlad hud a lledrith'*, anyway I'm out of
St Brides Bay now in Ramsey Sound, this profoundly visible tidal
race can span round eight to eighteen knots on spring tides which
has spawned trials of a deltastream generator and the 'bitches
white water kayak rodeo', the infamous 'Bitches' series of rocks
claimed the lives of three of the lifeboat Gem's crew in nineteen
ten after themselves liberating the two man company of the
'Democrat' from the sea,

across the sound Ramsey Island retain the largest colony of grey
seals in southern Britain, red deer run free maintained by the RSPB,
St Justinian a hermit from Brittany friend and confessor to St David
established a holy cell here, it's conjectured he was murdered
ostensibly for his criticism of monastic superfluity, his body washed
up on the mainland and the charming story goes, he walked across
carrying his severed head under his arm, interned at Porthstinian
then finally laid to rest in the cathedral, allegedly two thousand
bodies of dead saints lie buried on the island, the rocky heights of
Carnllundain and Carnysgubor highlighted by the sun once served as
guiding miradors for ancient mariners

at Penmaen melyn there's vestiges of two copper mines the last
one sidelined in eighteen eighty three after JR's dubious fatality,
I selvage the top of two fine tarns and big eratics by Carn ar Wig,
away over the colourful caves of Ogof Felen and Ogof Goch in Maen
Bachau bay, then drift past the impressive crescentic rampart and
ditch of Castell Hienif,

above the natural arch by Ogof Mary headland a murder of ravens
seen over on a byway signpost stir raving visions of *'the dream of
Rhonabwy'* host King Arthur playing *gwyddbwyl* with Owain, on past
St Justinians carn to the lifeboat station at Porthstinian and the
cadaver of *Capel Stinon* and sacred well, its purloined bell dropped at
sea is said to knell during a stormy mêlée, In eighteen ten Richard
Fenton who lived near to here at Rhosson wrote his 'Historical Tour
Through Pembrokeshire',

up and around Ynys Dinas, to Porth Brag where oddly a solitary
oystercatcher is perched on the crag, then past the lovely Porth
Hyfryd to the crevasse geo Porth Cadnaw and the headlands of
Penrhyn Dalar and Point St John's precambrian spill of columnar
dolerite and sill, then over a morass patched with desultory twill
grass to Maen Cam, above Ogof Cwm another fuzzy field of plum
scuzzy ponies and a fog born glum view of Carreg-gafeiliog,
according to the world map annals I've left the sound for St George's
channel, at the serene scene of Porthselau beach I cross the stone
pont and take a coffee break on the green sandstone font, I've a
hunch it's where Blanch Williams in seventeen eighty launched her
little clinker-built barque in a storm to save Swedish sailors stranded
on the Clerks,

a climb up again to Ogof Barfau round the craggy landmass of Carn
Llwyd past Ogofgolchfa to end the day at White Sands Bay, where
'Sailor Billy' a.k.a. William IV would dock to pay a visit to Mrs Jordan
at Treleddyn farm, to the right of this tranquil bight is St David's City
golf club, St Patrick had the nub of a vision here, to convert Ireland, a
primeval forest of beech, oak, hazel and fir is visible on very low
tides, where remains of aurochs and brown bear were found, the
site of my childhood nightmares the grand bad bellowing giant genie
thumping along the sand in 'the thief of Bagdad', nearby was the
abode of composer Thomas Tomkins who versed his composition
for the coronation of Charles I, at Trwynhwrddyn's lingula flag rock
'the elevator' serves as a popular dais for radical regular-footed and
paddlepuss surfers,

13. Some Profanities White Sands Bay—Porthgain

it really is a George Herbert *"sweet spring full of sweet days"* this
morning's bright awakening under the lucent gaze of a blue welkin,
with a clear sighting of the white lighthouse on *Em-sker*, yesterday
the Island array, erased by a dense haze fired a reflective blaze on the
brave Vikings navigating that perilous palaeozoic rock maze which
has claimed so much latter-day shipping such as the 'Morna' which
hit North Bishop carrying Irish recruits raised for the Crimea, even
induced Ptolemy's phrase in 150AD 'of the eight perils', and
Elizabethan George Owen's graceful reference, 'the Bishop and his
Clerks preach deadly doctrine to their winter audience'

back up above the tuff stack on Porth Lleuog beach along the track
to Crag y Creigwyr, beyond Penlledwen cape a sidetrack leads inland
and a trek up to the dolmen on Carn Llidi Bychan, where I check
by scant signs of 'highwinds' hydrophone submarine spotting station
from world war one, I strip off my backpack to replenish this weary
somatotype with coffee and a pipe while I wallow in the view to
Wicklow Mountains in Southern Ireland, replacing my haversack
I backtrack down to reach Portmelgan beach the scene of a fated
maritime saga of denigrated wreckers in sixteen sixty eight when the
Amity was breached, decked with her freight of wine from Malaga,
on a tragic late December night evocative of a great du-Maurier
classic, past more large eratics and an iron age fort to Ogof Gefr on
the stony arenig outcrop that is Penmaen Dewi or St David's Head

I think I'm standing at the exact location John Caxton extracted his
pastel and ink depiction in the forties, drawn here joining Graham
Sutherland who stated this coast was *'the place I began to learn
painting'*, on the ledge there's a grave memorial plaque for a
photographer swept off by a wave, I clamber back over the rocky
track to Ogof Cristal an a-lister with able climbers although you'd
never guess with labels like *'the headbanger'* and *'act of insanity'* and
then some profanities,

I trek to the dramatic cromlech *Coetan Arthur*, hike round the site of 'warriors dyke' and the stone circles it abuts marking out eight iron age huts, past LLechenhinen in then to the quartz ribbons of Carn Porth-Llong, and sped along to Porth Llong highest point on St David's Head where there was once a coastguard lookout shed, on to Maen Porth-Llong over the spall of an iron-age defensive wall to the headland of Trwyn Llwyd, and in so far as Porth Uwch on the eastern spar of the peninsular, walking on I pass into Cardigan Bay formerly a landmass cay home of *'Rhys of the Deep'* so the fables say,

I head past Dar y Cadno's narrow headland to Penllechwen and then the swan neck bending stream and spiralling shower wending it's way down to the accepting bay of Gesail Fawr swathed in gentle breakers, inland is a small walled passage to Maes-y-mynydd, in the mid sixteen hundreds a group of quakers escaping the injustice of unfriendly prejudice claimed a few acres and called it Pennsylvania, driven away by a typhoid epidemic or a poisoned well who can tell, on to Porth Coch and Trwyn Porth-coch, north then in towards Porthgwyn, at Penrhyn Halen there's an inland brow for a mile to Treleddyd Fawr cottage famously restoned by Gruff Rhys Jones,

on to Penrhyn Ffynnon-las, then Pig y Barcut and a tramp past Ogof Morlanod caves surveying Carreg yr Afr swamped by waves, over to Porth y Dwfr then more caves before Trwyn Dduallt gazing up at Carn Penberry and its disused quarry I step aside for an enthused couple jogging down from the aerie, while I stagger on round Penclegyr to Porth y Rhaw where a band of quarrymen swaggering sweaty and phlegmatic detraining to the shore to cool their callous, phlyctenae sore hands by a log rest on the corrade saw a phlogiston mermaid who proffered on them 'reaping in Pembrokeshire and weeding in Carmarthen', a happy rivalry we versed on the playing fields,

I go spinning off round Ogof Simmde beyond Porth Tre-wen a seaward stare met the Carreg-gwylan-fach and Ynys Gwair islet stacks, an iron age fort at Castell Coch, after Aberdinas a track leads back to Tremynydd Fach where I bivouac by Anna-Lou's sheepdog trial school, then head on over Stacen Barcutan and Trwyn Aber-pwll to scan the hedonistic milky-white cataract at Aber-pwll bight, the site of another hillfort at Caerau then disused quarries at Cyffredin and a tidy way down to the soft llanvirn shales and tuning fork graptolites of Abereiddy Bay where they're busily relaying the beach from the car park and slipway,

then away to the old flooded slate quarry that forms the blue lagoon where innate alary tombstoners lunged into the first dreadful UK red bull cliff diving competition, and Peter Cushing billed in 'the fury of smugglers bay' up the hill to the ruins of 'the street' lost to storm, disease and decay, past Abereiddi Tower meeting place or lookout? on Trwyncastell back inland to Gan Lŵyd and the old stone-quarry along Llyfn beach and the Cerrig Gwylan islets, I then peg over to Pen Porth Egr, above Porth Dwfn caves the view is so clear I almost stumble at the sight of Strumble lighthouse about fifteen miles up the coast, I rumble past Penclegyr head and the vast array of crumbling red brick working sheds and rusting tramlines, after Porth Ffynnon I aim for the declivitous steps leading down to Porthgain

Standing over this ordovician nappe fissure selecting the scenes of John Knapp-Fisher's affectingly candid canvasses from above the pilots house surveying the harbour's sunlit evening labour of fishing smacks and crews, now it's only commercial use other than a tourist aspect, unloading arthropod baskets of crab and lobster, aesthetic visitors congregate round the copacetic pubs, trademark cafés, galleries and hub of workmen's lorries by a jam-packed car park,

looking down on the brick and stone hoppers, it's instinctive to imagine the sthenic scene in years gone by with slate loaded trams from Abereiddi and related quarries, watermill gushers empowering slate saws then large steam crushers for road stone, yet it remains a pearl, completing this section I give the Sloop Inn a whirl to refuel and recoup in, when the slate industry buckled in eighteen seventy eight it left five hundred desperate quarrymen isolated for ages without work or wages

14. Afflatus to Write
Porthgain—Carn Ogof

back in Porthgain again amid a balmy late September eight oktas
cloud cover as I rotate, slide and amble through a hovering crowd, a
nexus of elderly ramblers, peevishly awaiting their late-in guide,
mischievously phonating a little mock sass as I overtake them on the
grass by the bridge making a fuss facing the steep snaking exodus,

I stop at the top by the bright white harbour marker and look across
at its somewhat cinereous sister, apparently their upkeep's
undertaken by opposing corporate protections, luckily the 'A' team's
taken off in the opposite direction, I pass the old quarry then around
Trwyn Elen into Gribanau bay surveying the caves on Ynys-fach the
islet stack painted in moody sunset by Max Oliver, on over Llanlleifer
to the waterfall in Pwllcrochan bay I stroll on along an area of daglock
stria path to the stone circle via the farm at Swyn-y-don although of a
contemporary era a well conceived idea, a celtic kalokagathia

a few blue cracks appear in an otherwise achromatic sky as I lope
down the sloping lane, by Aber Draw remain remains of a mill and
the spill of the stream that once powered it cowers down the hill in
the bay, the death of the miller gave 'Crwys' the afflatus to write the
famous poem, "Melin Trefin" a troop up this corniche avenue Trevine
village were cock-a-hoop when Cerys returned to the coop, along the
track is Aberfelin's Clychau stack's tideway tunnelled architrave cave,
a wooden bridge and wooden gateway convey me past a row of
cement rendered local slated cottages then the grey stone ruins of
the slate trade amid the ordovician grey nose headland of Trwyn
Llwyd, past Pwll Olfa over Pwll Llong and around Pwll Whiting
surveying a flock on the hill fort at Castle Coch then turning to view
the shore at Pwll Llong,

after refuelling a parch I get moving on to the natural arch in Ynys
Deullyn as I turn in at Cwm Badau and pace the ramp on to inspect
Carreg Samson cromlech I come face to face with *buteo buteo* the
brutish beauty of a common buzzard, briefly perched on a stanchion,
springs into flight expanding its substantial wings full span gives an
estranged mewing cry of goodbye then fans out of range,

apparently Saint Samson lifted the fifteen foot long capstone into
place using his finger, I linger awhile in approbation then saunter
along to Longhouse Farm once the daff grille fluxion for daffodil
production, I flank a fetching inspired feature of a retired teacher
sketching on the bank then crank down a grassy track and trail on
to the harbour past old canons placed as bollards all along the route
then incline to the old lime kiln examining Ynys y Castell guarding
the entrance to Abercastle quay, once used to control cargoes from
Bristol, where the *tylwyth teg* it's said patronised Iwan Llewellyn
with shillings, cheese and bread, in eighteen seventy six Alfred
Johnson landed traversing the Atlantic single-handed in a planned
observance to a hundred years of American independence,

a few miles inland is Letterston, whose name came from the
Fleming Letard Littleking when he was murdered for his sins by
Anarawd ap Gruffydd in the twelfth century his son Ivo granted the
village with some gramercy, *ecclesia villa letardi,* to the knight
commandery It's where Duffy's teenage years began...mercy,

I head up the steady gradient regaining the path adjacent to a large
stone ruin of a grainstore, then a tranquil view of the shore at Aber
Yw to the waterfall at Pwllstrodur, a curious seal scrutinizes my
presence in the bay, a popular spot for naturists here they say but
not this time of year, there's an inland pathway near that leads into
Mathry where a witch bewitched and cursed some cows, its quaint
church is dedicated to the seven saints,' y dyfrwyr', septuplets
raised on thaumaturgic fish by St Teilo who saved them when a
dramatic drowning in a sack would have done for them since their
traumatised parents lacked the means to do for them,

I hog the path by Aber Mochyn less known than its namesake in
Cuba, around Porth Glastwr to Trwyn Llwynog on the Mynydd
Morfa cape at its head is Penmorfa and Castle Coch rath with its
oscillating path, down by the old quarry there's a muddy track
through the foot of Pen-yr-Allt wood stretching back to Gilfach, on
to the pebbled beach of Aber Mawr and how amid the humidity of
sizzling summer in nineteen seventy, ensconced in an oddity of sea
surf boiling with a profundity of ammodytidae or sand eels Eric and
I fished a vast commodity of mackerel leaving a trail of scombridae
from one end of the bay to the other

the shoreline formed by Irish sea till, marine clays forced by ice, the
idyll site for Brunel's railway terminus a sacrificed tendril owing to
the disastrous Irish potato famine, scene of an illicit amphetamine
haul, a short sprint right leads uphill to the wall of Tregwynt's
seventeenth century mill and where a four hundred and eighty spill
of coins dated from the English Civil War was excavated, at Pen
Deudraeth there's recently vacated sand martin nesting holes,
as I look back a startling sea fret rolls in as I turn in to Aber Bach,

the telegraph shack was the terminal for the first trans-Atlantic
cable in the eighteen fifties, where a farmer waylaid a mermaid and
was cursed until he set her free, police discovered smugglers tanks
buried in the beach, over the stream up a steep track out of Aber
Bach around a hill fort looking over Carreg Golchfa, up here I'm
reminded of a precarious clamber up the side of this bank, Eric and I
fishing one gentle night were stranded by the tide, what's it Dylan
said *good men, the last wave by* I resided that sanguine summer
with him and Gweneira up the lane in St Nicholas, the church there
has an impressive circa tenth century wheel head cross,

a profound catastrophe down there on Porth Dwgan when all hands
were dashed as the 'Charles Holmes' liner demasted and smashed
forlorn in the great storm of eighteen fifty nine, as I take a gander
at Carreg Dandy I set eyes on another thin line of fine fog along the
horizon I padded past the greenschists facies ordovician metabasite
intrusions of Lech Dafad

on to the stock trusion bent arch at Porth Coch, high above gazing
inland I spy a clear skyline equine profile grazing on the rise, I heave
to Carreg Herefio then Pwll March, at Pwll Long a redwing just
arrived tapping it's prey upon the rock demands my attention as I
realign to Pwllcrochan sands' anticline formation, stacks and cave
erosions, on my way in to the inclined arch amid Trwyn Llwyd
murmuring seals and pups clog every indentation and alcove as a
wave of radiation fog raves along the coves,

up by Pwlldawnau sited over Cerrig Gwynion annihilated by mist
cover, to Aber Cerrig-gwynion I glimpse the polygonal columns at
Penbwchdy, pondering these polygenous forms like Friedrich's
'wanderer' as the last mists settle eerily carpeting the bays in haze
there's still a stencil silhouette gaze of Carn Penberry and Carn Llidi
on St David's Head, Carreg Bwch-du is immersed as I scurry off to
Carn Ogof setting my tent at its dada I brew myself some java, a
short hop inland is Trefasser birthplace of Meneventsis Asser,
nephew of Alfred the Great's flattering scribbler, In July o' nine, a
body was found along the shoreline at the base of these heights.
settling in for the night amid a stunning sunset paradigm, the
chromatic spectra and dramatic patterning from Mie and Raleigh
scattering that sparkle and shine like speckled chrome through
elevated cumuliform is truly, deeply sublime,

15. Rock Cycles Carn Ogof—Goodwick

emergent at dawn with the remnant of a split tent pole after last
nights convergent squall a quick breakfast all packed I'm back on
track scrambling over Carn Ogof in a lavender mist overlooking
Carreg Gerwynau very soon I'm at Dewi Emrys' memorial stone at
the cauldron that is Pwll Deri, the gorse is still spilling it's sovereigns
but no sign of Dai Breca on the beach below me, looming behind
me is the opulent mound of Garn Fawr climbing up I steer around
by Tal-y-Gaer medieval hermits 'hut' near the youth hostel, past
columns of volcanic dolerite then further up to the striking hillfort
occupying the scraggy outcrop where builders signed the
foundations of a first world war lookout post, the names of the
outposts officers are added in stone, down below is the cottage of
John Piper who painted this rugged cone over and over again

down and over to another hillfort extrusion and the quartz like
Igneous intrusion of micro tonalite sill in Dinas Mawr overlooking
Ynys y Ddinas, Ynys Melyn, Carreg Ddu the hole in Ynys Ddu then
out to Tri Maen-trai where troublesome waves try to swallow them,
the 'SS Vendome' hit these rocks and went down lost in a night-
time supersaturation, the crew oblivious of their position took to
boats, shamed faces at dawn and still afloat they rowed ashore and
saw where they'd landed, the master hailed from St David's and
sailor Joseph Garnon was an ex-piscator from Fishguard harbour,
forward around Penrhyn Byr to Porth Maenmelyn and the
precipitous steps cut into the mudstone cliff face, the north side's
volcanic rhyolite is overlaid with pillowed basalt lavas that structure
most of the phizog along this sector, a gentle push to Pen Brush,
then I plough on over March Mawr,

in to Pwll Arian, again the customary sight of grey seals in every
nook and cranny, above is the distended bird observatory opened
by Bill Oddie, over the hillier soddy rise to the mammilla simile Carn
Melyn, traces of blue and white recover the daylight skies at the
site of caves in Pwll Ffyliaid on then to Carreg Onnen Bay and the
imposing rock cycle spread and islet array of the lighthouse on Ynys
Meicel at Strumble Head, a hot spot for dolphin spotters, there was
a lot of U-Boat activity in this vicinity throughout world war two, I
trot on a jot on a rough tilth track around Pwll Bach

stubby tussock grass and gorse over Carreg Gybi whose patronymic
was celtic saint Cybi who apparently emerged from the sea on a
horse, he rejected the throne of Cornwall to go on as cleric, a jog on
around relics of stonewall to Pwlluog bay at last the ground fog's
clearing away, I pan down in inanity to Porthsychan's shingle beach
and up in a single breach of urbanity to reach Cnwc Degan the knoll
of saint Degan another celebrant grace, at Penrhyn by a lonely
cottage near Pen Globa was a sailors dedicated chapel to this
venerated but dapple saint yet no trace of it remains, an inland lane
heads south to Pen Caer, said to be where Culwych from the epic
account of the Twrch Trwyth lived, around Y Globa Fawr I race past
Carn Llwyd fluidly to Trwyn Llwyd and on then to Carn Halen

past the memorial stone to the last invasion of British mainland soil
at Carreg Goffa, on Carregwastad was the tougher French landing in
seventeen ninety seven after a failed attempt at Fishguard harbour, I
wander round Cwm Felin a path leads in to the compelling church of
St Gwyndaf in Llanwnda where I ponder a tattered Welsh bible dated
sixteen twenty that was liberated by latter day crusaders from the
denigrated French invaders,

back up to view the fissure of Aber Felin's natural arch and impelling
caves over which I gaze the StenaLine Ferry on its nautical labour to
Fishguard Harbour, some calcareous flora passing Pant y Bara, in
from Pant y Dwr I saw horses on Ciliau Moor their grazing is part of
the plan for this area of coastal heathland, shaving invasive scrub and
saving imperative shrubs, now trudging heavily with the weight of my
pack over Carnfathach and Maen Jaspis, from Penfathach through to
Porth Maen, around Y Penrhyn and Anglas Bay to Pen Anglas the
complex rock types Interlay with lavas, basalt volocaniclastics,
rhyolite, banded dacite, and intrusions of dolerite, near the head of
Pen Anglas there's a small marker and foghorn shed, the dolerite
here have four to six sided staves similar to those on the Giant's
Causeway and Fingals Cave,

on to Crincoed and circling Pwll Hir a trot over Pen-cw where the
stock schooner 'Charlotte' from out of Portmadoc was irretrievably
fated carrying a cargo of slate it lay splintered over the Cow and Calf
in a howling draught, all hands were saved from certain ruin by the
gallant exploits of the brave crew in the Fishguard lifeboat

at Goodwick I make for the cannons high above the north breakwater
raised on waste rock from the construction of the harbour, I'm at the
juncture over Brunel's 'old sheds' railway structures that boast a
'Blue Peter' seven lifeboat in the lower paraphernalia of buildings,
this dock once hosted the Mauretania before the silt settlings

I delve down through the park, in nineteen twelve a benchmark first
successful flight from the mainland to Ireland let fly from here,
some nervy mirth over the very high galvanised footbridge above
traffic from the ferry now berthed, back inland behind the Harbour
Village are three more cromlechs or *coitan* at Pen-rhiw Fach, at the
local beach of Goodwick Sands the rendered French attack force
amassed prior to their surrender of course,

I conclude the day's long trog by the 'Ocean Lab' ambling along the
'Parrog' in a dribbling fog, if you follow the road due south from here
past Tre-boeth you come by the Gate Inn in the tranquil setting of
Scleddau, fated to be the focus of the first defined tollgate attack in
eighteen thirty nine some imply it was a prelude to the rectitudinous
Rebecca Riots

16. Specular Reflection
Goodwick—Cwm yr Eglwys

a short intro note, the reverent reverend Thomas wrote in 'the view from the window' vis-à-vis the ever shifting scenery I quote *'these colours are renewed daily'* ergo I denote the last time I fraily trogged along the Parrog it was inclement, dark and drizzling, today's brilliant, buoyant, stark and sizzling chromatic imbuement emote the case in point, the sky a blue trivet broadsheet with the tightest stipple effect reflected on a blue velvet bed sheet sea with just the slightest ripple except way out where separated by a thin white strip on the horizon

the full power of the rising sun has still to scour the crown of the hills, prolonging the west bank's early November morning chill, prodding past the tranquil east breakwater, armed with my owl carved country stick *'Arianrhod'* a perquisite from brother Hywel, are some mallards oystercatchers, swans and a spoonbill, continuing on the tarmac path uphill around Penyraber a tendril of upper Fishguard at the spill of the river Gwaun, further on the Royal Oak pub was the site of the French capitulation drill with Lord Cawder at the head, and rendered with Clive Owen in 'I'll sleep when I'm dead' the town hall hangs a tapestry illustrating the French attack, there's a memorial plaque to Jemima Nicholas who singlehandedly captured a dozen niggardly troops after their balked assault at the skilled point of her pitchfork, hometown of nineteenth century vicar and historian Arthur Wade Evans, where Cerys Mathews was schooled and venter to the Pepper's West Wales Arts Centre

As I round Saddle Point turning into lower Fishguard facing the lucent quay commencing my sural paroxysmic shuffling decent, speculating the panoramic scene a spectacular specular reflection of the rural fleet on a current free water, and phototropic clatter muffling trees encircling *y cwm* swathed in smoky vapour following the sun's ascent a curlew stands guard as I drift by the jibbing boatyard, in the glib seventies render of Under Milk Wood this was Llareggrub, featuring a certain Richard Burton and a depiction of New Bedford 'call me Ishmael' in Melville's 'Moby Dick', with Gregory Peck's Captain Ahab, but at night where Bal's black dog lies in wait to grab your soul, a lighter seagull cavalcade stroll round the harbour is John Cleal's 'Sgadan Abergwaun' sculpture marking its bygone maritime herring trade,

up the valley, in Cwm Gwaun, they still prefer the Julian calendar and merrily observe *Hen Galon* on the thirteenth of January, home to the *cwrw cwm gwuan* brewery's good bitter, a good bit further on by Scleddau is Pantywrach where manganese was mined in the late nineteenth century, a short climb on to the cannon array of Castle Point Fort created here since a foray by the privateer Paul Jones in the 'Black Prince' made them pay, later on a volley aimed at the French assault ship fortuitously scared them away adscititlously they only had another three rounds to spare on the affray,

off then to Carreg Coffin, in my childhood a tuppenny boat trip would convey you to the coffin on the crag, as daybreak makes it to Carreg Tomas it's chock-a-block with a flock of kittiwakes loudly exclaiming their name, on a bit more to Porth LLandu's pebbled shore, high above in a field sparkling with morning dew by Parc y Morfa a cow and calf pasture as if to mirror their rocky namesakes on the other side of the dock, around Coch y Ceiliog and the cave below Garn Lwyd as I pass Y Das viewing the fissure that looks like an eyehook in Needle Rock and feature two razorbills on its top, inland are the denuded formatted earthwork hillocks of Carn Fran or crow hill and the stony zenith of Carn Gelli above the gently wrapped reef off Aber Richard beach adjacent to Cnwc y Meirch is a frightening lurch to the long pebbled beach of Pwll y Blewyn, I skew in to the clifftop caravan park at Penrhyn Ychen most of its buildings are a re-fashioning of first world war lookout posts, and six inch coastal artillery battery from the second, rocket launcher bases and corresponding searchlight emplacements can still be found, a slog around another pebbled beach below on Aber Grugog where all agog out to sea a motorboat skipping faster through the flatter waters like an unzipping zip fastener, around the excrescence of Penrhyn Mawr the presence of a fattening herd of Welsh Blacks scour the grassy banks as I veer into Aber Hywel named after my brother Huw....well that's not really true

bending to view a stock hillfort at Penrhyn Erw Goch with its crumbling blockwork like rock, sheep grazing in the field above cast unorthodox long shadows in the low lux late autumnal equinox, over Carreg Pen-Las the pass enters a shadowy hawthorn berry tunnel then corkscrews down to a komorebi meadow stream's afflux onto Aber bach's shore, a coffee and pipe of amphora's in order, amidst the usual perusal from a seal studying my arrival,

back up above the black rock Cerrig Duon and curved beach of Pwll Gwylog on then down to the wooden bridged stream in the golden bracken valley at Cwm Gwylog, as I shog up the slope amid a baleful mega chorus of gulls looking back at the cluster of black rocks resembling a herd of swimming stegosauruses, on my right flank ravens frolic on the bank in a sunbeam's light, that night in Rhonabwy's dream they were hoisting pageboys like toys to extreme heights then with a frightful lunge rejoicing at there dreadful plunge,

over a steep cutting and scree to the tiny pebbled beach at Pwll Cwm above which are some wind bent hawthorn trees, a dull plod down to the famous 'Old Sailor Inn' at Pwllgwaelod once graced by Dylan Thomas, another chance to settle with a flash demitasse of coffee as I rest and gather my mettle for the endurance test ahead, there was a fairy city under the sea at this bay, so folklore says with golden spires and marble palaces, once a local fisherman goofed while casting his anchor, a *dyn bach* climbed the cable complaining it'd holed his roof,

the ascent starts with a gentle climb to the hillfort at Pen Castell
overlooking Carreg-y-Fran at Pen Sidan then on to Pen-Clawdd and
Aber Carreg-y-Fran's shingle shore viewing the dramatic rock folding
at the northern end of Aber Pensidan around Cafnau high above Aber
Pen-clawdd to the ordinance survey triangulation viewpoint station
on Pen Y Fan, at Dinas Head the highest steep, four hundred and sixty
six feet, on Dinas Island, the scene south's a mountain skyline as
Mynydd Dinas rises, slightly left Carningli espouses Newport town,
reaching up to a Preseli backdrop where the blue stones of
Stonehenge came from, in clear skies the Cadair Idris, Snowdonia and
the Lleyn Peninsula can be seen from here

it's continuous downhill above Llech Isaf cave past the tremendous
geological folds at the vertiginous green pool, Pwll Glas, I dwell for
some guillemots on Needle Rock then on over Ogof Pig-y-mél cave to
Aber Trwyn scanning the spinous fin of Careg John Evan then panning
to Aber Pig-y-baw and pegging in to complete a days spruce-ish walk
at Cwm-yr-Eglwys

the apparent apparel of this little settlement is what remains of St
Brynach's sailors chapel its double arched bell-cote from a connote
Norman refurbishment denoted in fine oils in eighteen thirty one by
Henry Gastineau prior to its deathblow by the 'royal charter' storm of
eighteen fifty nine, there's a wooden depiction of a coastal trader at
the entrance to the graveyard which serviced the villages for ages,
before the construction of a sea wall bones and coffins were prone
to exposure by hefty wave action, the annual regatta is a popular
attraction with families taking part in a whole days events, from
swimming and rowing races to sandcastle building contests, this
sheltered cove has its own microclimate warmer and dryer than most
other parts of the coast this allows the growth of shrubs and trees of
almost Mediterranean luxury,

17. Fifty Shades Cwm-yr-Eglwys—
Ceibwr Bay

after yesterday's distended blue sky albeit the lank penny sundisc hadn't transcended the obelisk of western banks any, this morning's disparate, grisaille palette, perhaps not fifty shades but they rank many, flayed with azure, violet and a tiffany bisque tease in the mix, each shuffled along on a brisk breeze, after a short uphill interval along the road I rediscover the coastal path down a hedged alleyway of sloe covered blackthorn bushes whose delicate white flowers once figured in the celtic *'gŵyl fair y canhwyllau'* festival

I follow the whiskered path round Trwyn Isaac to the wizard hat Stack at Ynys Dol-rhedyn turning away into Aber Fforest pebbled bay at the hollow holocene estuary of a forested valley, over the lengthy wooden bridge past the limekiln on the slate cobbled ridge, this cove was also set alight by the palette of pre-Raphaelite John Brett, a spout exhales as I scale the eastern cliffs and travail the stepped mud plank embankment to the dank dark ordovician shales of a wave forged beach at Aber Ysgol around Penrhyn y Fforest and down to Aber Rhigian's protean pebble ridgebank and on over the lucid, sated stream on the divaricated V-shaped bridge clasping my fatigued *vastus lateralis* as I clamber the perpendicular siltstone path amidst some spectacular wind soaked contort of tormented oaks, inland through Cwm Rhigian are the five cists of the neolithic chambered tomb of Carreg y Gof 'the blacksmith's stone', then off over the wave cut platform at Traeth Brodan's steep cove to Aber Step's specular bending cataract facet facing Cat Rock at the head of another raised bed Traeth Samuel, an old protracted track cut in the bank backed with a hand rail descends from Carreg Germain down to the rocky shore, on past the host of oarweed and broken shells along Afon Nyfer accompanied by a plethora of shore birds and waders separating the parrog traders from the vast tract of sandy beach, Newport Sands, where *knappan* was played on Shrove Tuesdays against the parishers of Nevern, the river is breached by a giant sand bar, the Bennett as I pass the antecedent lifeboat station at the Cwm there's some willow sculpture on the marsh as I near the boat club,

the first humans, mesolithic settlers to land in north Pembrokeshire landed at Newport *Novus burgus* the town was founded in the twelfth century by William Fitzmartin as capital of the Norman marcher lordship of Cemaes after his concise ejection from his stern father's castle in Nevern, his first bastion was probably a riverside motte and bailey now known simply as *hen castell* eventually he rebuilt on the northern tilt of Carn Ingli, the fastigium for Brian Johns 'angel mountain' saga the site of St Brynach's communion with angels, there's remnants of bronze and iron age settlements here, John Seymour self sufficiency pioneer farmed at Fachongle on the eastern hills, where he scribed his book 'About Pembrokeshire',

shipbuilding and a sea trading parrog augmented the town 'til the mid nineteenth century, the castle gatehouse and walls were converted into residence halls acquainted by John Brett when he painted the scenery for miles around, hometown of Dillwyn Miles, poet, politician, adventurer and author of 'Portrait of Pembrokeshire'

I take a short deviation to check by Careg Coetan Arthur cromlech before I return to the iron bridge, crossing its deck over the Nyfer by the medieval *cerig-camud* stillage, a little further on is Llwyngwair village once home to James Bevan Bowen founder of the heraldic Bowen knot, the earnest host to evangelist John Weseley, another mile back easterly is Nevern church dedicated to St Brynach, the site of his sixth century 'clas', a vital tenth century high cross and the Vitalianus Stone dated from around 500AD, there's also a 'bleeding yew tree' that leaks red sap perhaps lamenting for a young man wrongfully hanged or it will weep until a Welsh prince rules this land, another that it will cease when the world is at peace, George Owen of Henllys High Sherriff and author of 'The Description of Pembrokeshire' is buried here,

on then past the Limekiln at Shiphill by Ffynnon Bryncyn through the links golf course, above the vast protean sandbank to Cesig duon's chevron anticline in turbidite ordovician mudstones and sandstones folded during the caledonian oregeny, past the navigation beacons, at Pen Pistyll is Brynach's waterfall, up the long stacked staircase at Cyfrwy to Bal bach's petite beach, the black rocks here have fine web like igneous intrusions from magma seepage as I reach Pen-y-bâl looking in at the caves,

I clamber up more steep wooden staves at Maes Ffynnon to Pen Cafnau above ogof drwy then a stone track upward to a lofty five hundred feet by a concrete marker marking a cairn where I mark Mr Lewis's farm at Morfa-uchaf, round Pen Morfa with an overview of the long spattering ridgeway of islets that is Carregedrywy, past Godir Tudor bearing up to Godig Mawr staring up further to the peak of Foel Fach and another iron age enclosure, back at Godir-y-bwch taking a look at the unsteady scree rolling down to the rock eddied sea,

while circling the sandy ring of Godir Rhyg I met with several badger
sets, badger forever homologous of Grahame's judicious character
is endemic for me, yet smouldering images of cattle linger infected
with TB, and that, after another epidemic of FMD, farming here is
generally mixed like it's support i.e. prices fixed, European fiscal
policy without a common currency, while eighties administration
strategy mistakes gave us butter mountains and milk lakes but our
moderate climate diktat born on Atlantic currents, that Gulf stream
keeps the steeps of Preseli studded with sheep, the dry sandy coast
seeping early potatoes, the fructiferous valleys, gulches and arroyos
stocked to the top with game, livestock and crops, of course the best
barley and wheat it's said was bequeathed to us by Dallwyr Dallbed
at Llonion or Llanion as in the chronicles of Hen Wen,

On then to Trwyn y Bwa or calf's nose high up over those hidden
caves round Godir-y-Golomen pulsated by the fresh wind
discombobulated sea, I'm cursing the swampy pathway when I'm
suddenly confronted with the guilty party, half a dozen unruly ponies
above the little bay of Pwll Goch, on to Gerddi-bâch to my left is
Slipping incline sharply sloping to the waters edge, to my right is the
higher Foel Gôch and a hedged inland walk to Castell-y-garn bulwark
and the dolmen at Trellyffaint, Gerald of Wales allegedly told tales of
rapacious toads that came, attacked and ate a man hung from a tree
in a sack, a vain fount to account for its name,

down and across the orthogonal stepping stones at Ffynnon Coeg
then on to Cell Howel, well below is the lengthy shingle beach of
Traeth Cell-Howel to the eventual arrival at Ogof Cadno and Cyfrwy,
inland up on the neck of Llech y Drybedd 'stone of the three graves'
lays a cromlech with a large wedge shaped capstone, quicker back
down overlooking Carreg Bica, the ridge up here has the telltale
perforations of sand martin habitation, I ramble off to Ogof Goch
looking back at the arch that resembles a cup handle at Bwn Bach,
the wind booms and the sea fumes passing the gruff ridge of
Castellreruffydd iron age fort a teardrop shaped enclosure where a
Roman pot sherd was discovered, clinging on past Cwm Ffynnon-
alwm's chalybeate spring looming into Traeth Bach with its loose
shale cliffs an obtuse analysis as far as Careg Yspar and the abyssal
geo before the witches cauldron Pwll y Wrach a massive blowhole or
gloup with a natural loop arch and potholes then the tricky narrow
track extended along its ridged back like a bridge where I stand and
watch a peregrine chasing pigeons as the waves cascade beneath me,

before racing on to another fissure and row of jagged teeth stacks at
Careg Wylan on to Ceibwr Bay with its classic array of intricate
harmonic folds and faults in the multifaceted bands of dark
mudstones and iron rich sandstones, where the Morning Star out of
Aberystwyth was another victim of that defining storm of eighteen
fifty nine, a black trade of Cherbourg cognac was carried out at this
haven in eighteen seven, the villagers were all in seventh heaven 'til
the contraband liquor maddened the vicar,

18. Embracing the End Ceibwr Bay—St Dogmaels

a notable day at Ceibwr Bay still absurdly struggling with the now common donning of my hiking belongings on the tail of my car seeming extremely far from that mammoth October dawn at Amroth, It's hard to accept on this windswept November morning's muted light blue sky becoming paler even white as it loses height kissing the sea at a concealed division on the fringe of my field of vision, that I'm facing, embracing the end, one last day to spend on my quest along this curvilineal coast, I cross the current granite clapper bridge constructed after concurrent dapper versions collapsed, rent asunder many times culminating in the June ninety three torrent when eleven centimetres of rain fell in four hours and the ensuing current completely washed it away,

I track up the steady gradient at Ynys Fach around the hillfort to Pen-castell past the caves along Dwr Nel then a bending path over Foel Hendre stood above Cadlan Valley prize winning stud at Hendre farm, back along the undulating coastline a sheer slant to the footbridge across the Granant that springs up at Cippyn fawr tumbling on via Cwm yr Esgyr and Gernos cascading on to Pwllygranant, following the northbound curvature round Traeth y Rhedyn dreading the snaking view ahead of a long sloping incline weighing up the hard groping climb towards Cyfrwy then up and up again to Pen yr Afr 'goats head' five hundred and seventy five feet boast of the highest point on the whole of the coast, scanning back to the light beam on Strumble Head panning to and fro then speeding on to Carreg Lion and Pwll Tro as the cloud cover spreads and it starts raining, the sheep in the field line up sheltering against a hedge in defence giving the appearance of straggling wool balls dangling from a barbed wire fence,

a consortium of atlantic grey seals adorn the long diluvium shingle
beach of Traeth Godir-côch where there'll soon be an imposing
symposium during the winter moult, high above the clouds break and
a colourful rainbow spectrum reflecting on the blue cadmium sea
augments the amazing patterning of rock stratum in Craig yr Odyn,
the wind joins in as I steadily climb to the old lookout shed standing
on the lofty podium of Cemaes Head the northernmost promontory
on the Pembrokeshire coast, stretching towards Ceredigion the
largest European colony of bottlenose dolphins can be found, around
July, August if your lucky, and don't blink there's august sightings of
orca and even Minke,

along a slender strip of mud path. enjoying the effects of this
naturopath walk knowing that was the very last hill, the closing
stages approaching to soon, still below is King Road and Pwll y Mwn,
at the entrance gate I start downhill edging Cemaes Nature Reserve
following the path right shadowing a robin down the light ramp until
facing a damp view of Cardigan island then turning in to the moraines
and sand of the Teifi estuary joining the loam path over Careg Aderyn
and Ogof Gröyn to Allt-y-goed farm and campsite quickly over Careg
Lydan and Pwll Edrych,

from here a small oak lined road propelling me past Pwll Melyn,
along by Trwyn yr Olchfa and Penrhyn Castle passing the breakwater
at Cei-bâch a facile arrival at the shore by Trwyn Careg-ddu with its
sandstone and siltstone debris, mudstones and turbidites, further on
a flight of gaggling Canada geese alight along the beach to join the
already crowded selection of wildfowl including heron, shags and
mallards, on to the lifeboat station where the path takes me towards
the dunes over Poppit Sands' raised beach, soon I reach the old end
of walk signpost for once I'm almost happy to report they've moved
the goalpost,

my extrication organised as I near the end, some boffin hypothesised that if we send carbon dioxide into the air, by the way this isn't a scare, it disguises the greenhouse effect by suppressing drizzle inflect well so they say, that's certainly not the case today, up the hill here Albrow Castle was a workhouse for the poor until it housed a US military corps, then dealt with war child evacuees it once became flats for lease, then condemned and left to decay, now you can book it for your holidays,

I've been walking factually naturally along this trek recounting the early years, recollections, damp lamentations some smouldering regrets although not old or decrepit enough yet to think I can't enjoy them again with respect for accrued knowledge and aged wisdom replacing first time excitement and expectation,

I reach St Dogmaels by the quay on a little cay near where ruins of the abbey lay, here every summer they feature a Shakespeare play, St Thomas church houses the Sagranus stone used in deciphering Irish ogham, I arrive at the new end of walk plaque by the mermaid figurine then dump my pack, the damp flag, *Baner Cymru* pummelling in a glum sideswipe squall of high wind,

the late afternoon sprawling low lulled Teifi crabbing the muddy sands and still a phon of squawking seagulls over me struggling to strip my bland walking garb in a cheerless November drizzle senses waning aching muscles troubling me, I moan and grizzle yet I survived my feat of certitude through the seasonal solitude trying to balance in the gloaming against the car boot on gravel and stone in stocking'd feet I'm yawning, chilly damp and soggy, frail and tender behind lays hilly ramp and boggy dale I've reached the end.